The Creative Workplace

ROADS Publishing
19–22 Dame Street
Dublin 2
Ireland

www.roads.co

First published 2016

1

The Creative Workplace

Text copyright
© ROADS Publishing
Design and layout copyright
© ROADS Publishing

Designed in Ireland by WorkGroup
Print manufactured and managed
by Jellyfish Solutions

British Library Cataloguing
in Publication Data
A catalogue record for this book is
available from the British Library

978-1-909399-79-2

The Creative Workplace

R O A D S

PUBLISHING

Workplaces

Introduction

Rob Alderson

It's trite to say that the creative process is mysterious, but that doesn't make it any less true. Any visit to a creative space – whether a large multinational design agency or a desk in the spare room of a freelancer friend – becomes a snooping expedition. From the books on the shelf to the choreography of the desktop, the prints on the walls to the music, light and temperature – all of these clues feed into the key question: how does all of this help you do what you do?

Creativity is difficult to define and almost impossible to describe. As graphic designer and Pentagram partner Paula Scher puts it: 'I can describe all the stimulus – your experiences, the books you've read, the art you've seen, the movies you love. All these things are rolling around on one side of your brain, and on the other side there's your brief and the brief is like a quarter. You put your quarter in the slot machine and if you're lucky three cherries line up and you've solved the problem. If you're not lucky, you're struggling.'

But to struggle isn't sexy, and so we continue to be fascinated by that triangular relationship between the creative, their work and their space, poring over the evidence to try to untangle how each factor affects the others. Sometimes, the spaces we come across don't look anything like we might expect: such is the very personal nature of the slot machine described by Paula Scher. Andy Stevens, the co-founder of London-based graphic design agency Graphic Thought Facility, once said that clients 'wouldn't be tremendously impressed' with their space because it was designed for their creative needs rather than to 'look' creative – he drew a comparison between working farms and idyllic holiday farms.

Sometimes, though, these spaces look exactly as you'd expect. A couple of years ago, the *New York Times* reporter James B. Stewart visited Google's New York headquarters and his description reads like a satire on the archetypal twenty-first-century creative workplace. He found: 'a labyrinth of play areas; cafés, coffee bars and open kitchens; sunny outdoor terraces with chaises; gourmet cafeterias that serve free breakfast, lunch and dinner; Broadway-themed conference rooms with velvet drapes; and conversation areas designed to look like vintage subway cars. Next to the recently expanded Lego play station, employees can scurry up a ladder that connects the fourth and fifth floors, where a fiendishly challenging scavenger hunt was in progress. Dogs strolled the corridors alongside their masters, and a cocker spaniel was napping, leashed to a pet rail, outside one of the dining areas.'

Some of what Stewart describes sounds clichéd now, but it's important to remember that it was Google, alongside some of its big Silicon Valley neighbours, that first pioneered this kind of self-consciously creative workplace. And while some may cringe at the 'Broadway-themed conference room' and the 'Lego play station', Google has crunched the numbers. 'Like most of our decisions, data shows that these spaces have a positive impact on productivity, collaboration and inspiration,' its careers website says. So Google didn't embrace pet rails and free breakfasts because it was trying to be kooky; its data showed this was how to get the best out of its employees.

For creative agencies and design studios, workplaces are part of their brand identities, helping to attract and retain both creative talent and commercial clients. But there is a definite sense that there exists a direct cause and effect between the spaces people work in and their productivity, creativity and outlook. Google's data-driven workplaces may drive the idea to its extreme, but as Paula Scher articulates, the creative process is capricious and bloody hard. People will always shape their spaces to give them an advantage, building an atmosphere that helps them think and work in the best possible way. Scientific studies support this idea that getting into the right frame of mind is crucial, and this is as true for the 200-person advertising agency as it is for the lone illustrator.

In 2012, a team of researchers led by Allen Braun and Siyuan Liu studied the brains of rappers to see what happened when they were freestyling, or coming up with improvised lyrics. What they found – in simple terms – was that the areas of the brain linked to the decision-making process relaxed, allowing other areas connected to context, associations and emotional responses to fire into action.

Other researchers have pointed to the importance of distractions in the creative process. They say that it's often only when the brain focuses on something else that the elusive creative breakthrough can finally happen – this is why, they suggest, we often have great ideas in the shower or while out jogging.

And so, if science suggests that organisations can design and build spaces that allow for the right conditions in which creativity can flourish, then surely they'd be crazy not to try. The important thing is that they understand why they are doing it. It can't be a zany creative environment as an affectation, or a visual one-liner – more than one workplace has built a literal 'blue-sky room', complete with fluffy white clouds to encourage 'blue-sky thinking'.

An added complication is that creativity is a very individual thing. In 2013, I worked with design recruitment specialists Represent and It's Nice That on a project called The Ideal Studio, for which I interviewed twenty designers about what factors, both physical and organisational, contributed to an efficient and enjoyable workplace. Apart from good coffee (mentioned by almost everyone), the interviewees' responses were very diverse.

Take the idea of hierarchy. For obvious reasons, young companies like to throw off the shackles of the fuddy-duddy organisations around which they want to run rings, and so many of them like to mix everyone up together, with the CEO seated next to the intern. In theory, this sounds great, but in practice it can be a nightmare. The CEO now needs to wander off around the office if he wants a quick catch-up with his deputy, and the intern is overwhelmed by sitting next to someone so senior and is paralysed with fear from nine in the morning to six at night (five on Fridays).

Everyone works in different ways. Some people need complete silence to focus; others flourish in a raucous atmosphere and feed off that energy. Some people need thirty minutes at lunchtime to get out of the office and clear their heads; others adore the midday studio Pilates sessions. Some people need a tidy, clean space to order their thoughts and ideas, while we've all worked with a colleague whose desk resembles a Tracey Emin-esque artwork (sponsored by Pret a Manger).

Here again, an interesting tension appears when it comes to clients – anyone who has worked in a creative studio will have been told to clean up their workspace ahead of a big pitch meeting; the implication being that clients want to see creative workplaces, unless, of course, it's not a very photogenic kind of creativity.

Again, science may have some pointers on this matter. A team from the University of Minnesota did an experiment where they invited subjects into either a tidy or a messy room and asked them to come up with new uses for ping-pong balls. These ideas were scored by independent judges, with the messy group easily outperforming their tidy counterparts. As an example, while one of the messy group suggested using the balls cut in half on chair legs to protect floors from being scuffed, the best the tidy group could come up with was Beer Pong, a popular American drinking game that uses ping-pong balls, as, well, light, bouncy balls.

In the Ideal Studio project, some ideas did crop up consistently, most notably the benefits of happenstance. Many people I spoke to were convinced that some of the best ideas and the most natural forms of collaboration occurred in informal or unstructured ways; someone walking through the studio, spotting a design pinned up on a wall and initiating a conversation, for example, or chatting over beers. Google believes this is super useful too; so much so that the cafés are designed to build up queues at lunchtime during which time employees from completely different

sections might strike up potentially very useful chats (in Google terminology these are known as 'casual collisions').

It's tempting to dismiss the impact of workplace design with the Chuck Close quote – 'Inspiration is for amateurs, the rest of us just show up and get to work.' But in some ways, we are going back to the notions of inspiration and genius espoused in the Ancient World. Elizabeth Gilbert spoke about this in her excellent TED talk. Gilbert, who wrote a supremely opinion-splitting book called *Eat, Pray, Love* (later turned into a saccharine Julia Roberts film), explains how the Greeks and Romans thought of creativity 'as a spirit that came to human beings from some distant and unknowable force for distant and unknowable reasons'. This magical entity, she continues, 'was believed to live in the walls of an artist's studio … and invisibly assist the artist with his work'.

There may be more data and more science in play now, and more university research teams thinking about freestyle rap and ping-pong balls. But we still look to the walls (and the desks, and the Broadway-themed conference rooms) for any conceivable advantage in the hard daily battles – against cliché, against deadlines, against our own nagging doubts – that characterise the creative process.

Fingers crossed for three cherries.

3XN

Copenhagen, Denmark

3XN, a leading Danish architecture firm, relocated to its new 2,000-square-metre studio in December 2014. The staff of approximately eighty professionals now works in a historic former 'cannon boathouse' along a canal in Copenhagen's Holmen neighbourhood.

Design: 3XN
Photography: Adam Mørk

Our goal was to have one space in which all staff could see and interact with each other, as well as provide the best facilities for model-making. This historic boat shed, which dates from the mid-nineteenth century, was originally used to repair and store military boats. The floor slopes slightly towards the adjacent canal, which allowed the boat builders to slide the boats out into the water. The eastern façade faces the canal and is lined entirely with full-height windows and operable doors to ensure a well-lit work environment for all staff.

Kim Herforth Nielsen, 3XN's founder, believes that everyone has valuable ideas to contribute to our projects and the life of the firm. He designed the new studio to facilitate communication, laying it out as one open plan that locates staff based on their group.

It is a pleasure to watch the seasons change, see the play of light on the water, wave to passing boats, see birds and other creatures, and enjoy this serene setting in the heart of the city.

72andSunny

Los Angeles, USA

72andSunny is an award-winning agency that creates cultural impact on behalf of brands. The company moved to the Hercules Campus in the up-and-coming LA creative hub of Silicon Beach in 2013.

Design: 72andSunny & Lean Arch Inc.

Photography: 72andSunny

The agency specifically chose the former offices of famed aviator and film mogul Howard Hughes with the goal of continuing his legacy of creative innovation. To reimagine the space, which had been vacant for decades and had become a desolate property, 72andSunny enlisted the acclaimed architectural firm Lean Arch Inc. Together, the agency and the firm transformed the two office buildings into light-filled collaborative environments, while at the same time maintaining their historical foundation.

Displayed in the reception area is the authentic map of Hughes's original flight plans, which was found behind old drywall during the renovation. Employees sit at their own desks in very open work areas. There are no personal offices, and each open work area mixes departments and job levels. Various lounge areas are placed throughout both buildings, giving our employees a place to work other than their desks.

Howard Hughes's office was originally designed to represent the mogul's personality, and is used as an open workspace for the agency. One of our large conference rooms is built into his patent safe; the original steel door remains as an entryway, and rows of blueprint drawers and shelves line the walls that once housed the beginnings of some of his greatest creations.

Using UCLA's old hardwood basketball court floors from the 1980s, we built a giant auditorium for company meetings, events and screenings. The same hardwood was used to make the floor to our new locker room, which is lined with vintage blue school lockers.

Inside, the office also has a 'living wall', consisting of various plants and giant electric garage doors that open to a beautiful back deck, which is lined with 100-year-old sycamore trees.

Anthem Branding

Colorado, USA

A branding company based in Boulder, Colorado,
Anthem was founded in 2006 by creative
entrepreneur Ted Church. The company designed
their most recent office space with the help of
Surround Architecture, and the project was
completed in June 2014.

Design: Anthem Branding & Surround Architecture
Photography: Daniel O'Connor

We are located in beautiful Boulder, Colorado. After
planning, designing and building our dream space, we
moved into our current office in June 2014. We like to
think that we're different from other creative shops.
Our full-service advertising agency capabilities are
only half the story. We're also experts in the design
and production of impactful promotional products and
stylish consumer apparel.

We can tackle any challenge – from top-to-
bottom branding assignments to one-off promo item
production runs – and we do it for all types of clients,
from local start-ups to massive international brands.

We aimed to create an environment that fosters
collaboration, open communication and creativity
among our employees. The design of our space
balances an industrial edge with an organic feel,
incorporating 360-degree views of the mountains that
surround us. The open floor plan allows for simplicity
and increases the exchanges between every department
within the agency. We wanted to build a place where
our employees are inspired and enthusiastic to come
to work each day. The people that work here are an
incredible, passionate and brilliant team.

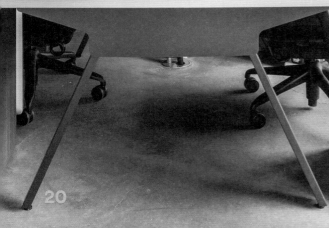

Barbarian Group

New York, USA

Barbarian Group is a tech-centric creative company that focuses on creative ideas and content. Founded in 2001 and located in Chelsea, New York, their award-winning office features a 'Superdesk', a 134-metre-long desk that curves around the workspace.

Design: Clive Wilkinson Architects
Photography: Michael Moran

The Barbarian Group, a new-generation internet advertising agency, required a workspace design that would foster collaboration and transparency in their growing company, and challenge their creativity. They leased a 7,000-square-metre loft in the New York garment district to house 125-175 Barbarians, which was surgically gutted to create a large open space.

Since conventional office tools are now largely redundant, people simply need flat surfaces to work on and easily accessible places to meet and collaborate. The company got excited about the idea of massively simplifying this concept by uniting all employees at a kind of 'endless table'. Like an electrical wire, the table surface itself becomes a medium for connecting and centring a community.

The plywood structure rises from the existing oak floor as pony walls supporting the table. Because the movement routes bisect the space, the table was lifted to fly over pathways and maintain surface continuity. The resulting grotto-like spaces underneath the 'arches' can accommodate meetings, provide private focused workspace or high counter workspace, and house bookshelves and other storage.

Bedow

Stockholm, Sweden

Bedow is a design studio located on Södermalm in Stockholm. The building, which was constructed in 1902, once housed a fire station and a police station, and Bedow's space is located in what used to be the policemen's locker room.

Design: Bedow
Photography: Bedow

Since we spend more than half of our lives at work, we want employees to be happy while being in the studio. That is the most important thing. I don't think we have a design concept, but we try to do as much as possible ourselves — from renovating and painting to furniture and pottery. It takes time, and, as you can see, this is an ongoing project. It's not very expensive but most objects in the studio have a history and together they create a nice atmosphere.

We're on the ground floor and often have our windows open, which lets us hear the most interesting conversations from the street outside. There are many good restaurants in our neighbourhood so we can have a decent lunch every day. It is important to leave the studio for a while so you can think of something other than work.

Bold-design

Paris, France

William Boujon and Julien Benayoun, the creative duo of Bold-design, launched their studio in 2008. Their office is situated on a 170-square-metre roof terrace in Paris.

Design: Bold-design
Photography: Marie Guerre & Bold-design

We redesigned a very old machine room on a roof terrace that previously housed a motor lift. The space is small and we like to think of it as a ship with an economy of means. It is small but functional, with almost anything you need to work, read, relax and meet clients. We took advantage of what could be seen as heavy constraints, such as the different levels of the concrete floor.

We have two favourite things about our workplace! The atypical size and location: we are on a rooftop which also means that, on a nice day, we have plenty of space to experiment, work or have a quiet lunch outside, even if we are in the middle of a noisy city like Paris. Then we managed to create a two-metre-long foam mattress hidden by trapdoors. We really think that changing your point of view or taking a quick nap is good for creativity, even if we don't take enough time for this.

Clients are always really surprised when they arrive on the rooftop of 'le 100' building and find us on the terrace with the garden, the view and the mural. They find it refreshing and an interesting atmosphere. They ask questions about how we managed to get there.

BUREAU Mario Lombardo

Berlin, Germany

BUREAU Mario Lombardo is an interdisciplinary design company based in Berlin. Its portfolio consists of design, artworks, original products and collaborations with selected designers, editors and photographers.

Design: Mario Lombardo
Photography: Mirjam Wählen

The concept for the office is a mixture of a Belgo-French restaurant and a design studio. In the centre of the office is the kitchen. The furnishings are very colourful and I've ensured that we use different chairs and different furniture elements. The workspace is separated by a colourful curtain. Everything is allowed in the other area: we cook and hold meetings there.

My favourite thing is the kitchen, because food, and especially the preparation of food, is the greatest metaphor for my work. And I love the curtain, of course.

Clients are all astonished by the working environment because we are located in the backyard of an industrial building in Kreuzberg. They are pleasantly surprised.

31

C&C Design Co. Ltd.

Guangzhou, China

C&C Design is a young, cutting-edge design company in Guangzhou. The creative headquarters of the company are situated in a post-industrial workshop.

Design: C&C Design Co. Ltd.
Photography: Ivy Photography & Production

The inspiration for the design comes from the tranquillity of nature. In terms of the spatial dimensions, the Chinese elements – bamboo and brick walls – have marked the region of the design, and the symbols of modern architecture – cement and glass – have endowed the design with modernity. Such a design integrates the materiality and affectivity of the space and constructs an environment of coexistence for the space and the people in it.

The building was transformed from a red-brick factory in the 1960s. In considering the protection of the current situation and the historical memory of the building, we have tried our best to avoid damage to the original structure in the renovation, and the 4.9-metre interior storey height gives us more space for our design. A lot of fir and bamboo are used in the interior. The opening and closing and the changeover of spaces are cleverly conceived. The lighting designs for different regions reflect different visual atmospheres.

Different spaces give people different feelings. The front hall, the passages and the meeting room give people a feeling of tranquillity and fineness. The public office area gives people a feeling of openness and freedom, while the water bar area gives people a feeling of leisure and relaxation. We hope that every space can further stimulate the inspiration of the designers working in them.

We cannot just *[unreadable]* to examine and *[unreadable]* own thought. The *[unreadable]* art, to question *[unreadable]* state of mind.

Casa Rex

São Paulo, Brazil

Casa Rex is an internationally acclaimed house of design, with a main office in São Paulo and a base in London. Their team of almost forty people has been in their current office for almost four years.

Design: Casa Rex
Photography: Rafaela Netto

The concept was to explore a combination of rough and raw materials – from the house's façade, built up from modular metal frames filled with rocks, to the bannisters made from construction sewer pipes.

Our favourite thing is probably the staircase at the back of our workspace – with a ceiling height of nearly seven metres, the wall has been entirely occupied by giant modular concrete blocks, one stacked on top of the other.

The bold exterior and unexpected structure tip off visitors to the building's raw concept, but the clearest reactions occur in the reception area, a room that almost looks like a demolition site. That always makes a positive first impression.

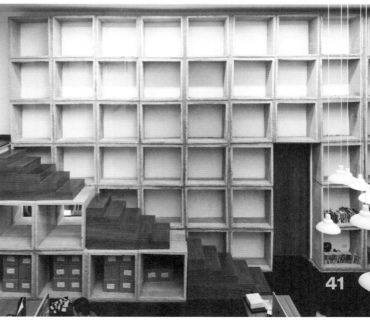

41

Carlo Bagliani

Genoa, Italy

Bagliani Ltd is an architecture and real-estate development company founded in 1999 by the firm's namesake, Carlo Bagliani. Their offices in Genoa were built in 2013, occupying 305 square metres of underground garage space.

Design: Sp10
Photography: Anna Positano with Nuvola Ravera

We realised this workplace by transforming an existing underground 'open space for art' designed in 2004 by my previous architecture office, 'Sp10'. We arranged a monolith in the middle of the large open space (in order to set our archive inside and also to determine two spaces on each side: one for workstations towards the big window, and one for technical equipment and a small kitchen on the other side); then we coloured everything in black and furnished with white desks and shelves, designed in-house by Sp10.

Our workplace, although located in the town, is a sort of haven where people feel better. It's wonderful during a squall to stay here in our underground shelter.

Clients and visitors are, at first glance, very surprised and a little unsettled by our office, perhaps because of its 'total black' appearance; but during the meetings, nearly everyone seems to enjoy the 'visual silence' and appreciates the opportunity to relax and concentrate at the same time.

Our workplace, although located in the town, is a sort of haven where people feel better. It's wonderful during a squall to stay here in our underground shelter.

Cutler

Vancouver, Canada

Cutler is an interior design and project management company based in Vancouver. It was founded in 2009 by husband-and-wife duo Jeff and Natalie Cutler, and the team moved in to their current workspace in 2014. The office is located in the historic Gastown district of Vancouver city, and it occupies 120.7 square metres of bright, open-plan workspace.

Design: Cutler
Photography: Luke Liable

Cutler wanted to highlight beautiful pieces that had the strength to stand alone. Our office design was more driven by the finishes and fixtures we loved, and how they made people feel in the space. This gallery-style office was and still is fuelled by a minimalist aesthetic, and continues to be warm, bright and inviting.

We had a splurge/save mentality, as we do in most projects. Examples of that being high-performance desks and chairs from Herman Miller that encourage efficiency and happy designers, while saving on millwork and materials with textured qualities (for example, printed wood graphics and whitewashed laminate flooring).

Our office is commonly referred to as 'The Treehouse', as we have two full walls of windows that look out onto the tree-covered Gastown streets. The thing about our office is that it feels quite residential. It reveals a professional setting but undeniably ends up being a place you want to kick off your shoes, a place you want to burn the midnight oil.

DekoRatio

Budapest, Hungary

Founded in 2003 by entrepreneur and brand strategist Peter Kremmer, DekoRatio is Hungary's first branding and design studio. The company is based in Budapest, where they moved into an office designed by KissMiklos in 2015. The office occupies 100 square metres, and is a playful mixture of industrial aesthetics and comic-book quirks.

Design: KissMiklos

Photography: Balint Jaksa

We wanted to create an experience that inspires ambitious companies to use better design and to demonstrate how design can have a huge positive effect on their business. That's why the number one goal was to design a space that offers a creative experience and serves as a showroom for interior design and decoration.

Several references to branding and the design profession appear around the studio: the Lorem Ipsum sign on the wall and the round meeting table that is designed as a big Pantone palette. The symbols of world-famous superhero characters are also a tribute to the extraordinary branding achievements of Disney, Marvel and DC.

In the library-style social room, the bookshelf was custom-made from the letters of LEARN, which is accompanied by a big 'Believe in BETTER' sign that abbreviates to 'Believe in BEER' as a sliding door opens across it.

Designed type with the studio's mottos, strategy and goals appear around the interior. They form part of the employer's branding effort, but they also give clients and other visitors a feel for the personality and values of the studio.

Designliga

Munich, Germany

Designliga is a bureau for visual communication and interior design. Founded in Munich in 2001 by product designer Saša Stanojčić and communication designer Andreas Döhring, the office has grown into a team of experienced designers, consultants and interior designers.

Design: Designliga
Photography: Designliga

Designliga took a former industrial machine shop and created a new working environment for its own staff and for Form & Code, its strategic partner in web and application development.

An industrial complex originating in the mid-twentieth century, the site has 650 square metres of hall space and visible traces of its previous use as a machine shop: an elevated foreman's office, once used for supervising shop-floor operations, tells a tale of order, streamlining and clear-cut hierarchies. For Designliga, this legacy of German industrialisation is a mirror reflecting the quintessence of work, and a motivation to examine the meaning of work in our contemporary age.

Dogpatch Labs

Dublin, Ireland

Dogpatch Labs is a co-working space dedicated to supporting entrepreneurship and a culture of innovation, and is at the forefront of supporting early-stage innovation in Ireland. Dogpatch is located in the vaults below Dublin's CHQ building in a redeveloped whiskey and wine store.

Design: Harry Browne & Daniel Moran
Photography: James Keating

We were actually presented with a truly unique opportunity to work within the constraining environment of the vaults here in the CHQ. It was important for us to respect the rich historic fabric of the space without, of course, creating a mausoleum to the past. We wanted to strike a balance between the robust nature of the vaults and the playfulness of the start-up community.

Our members' bar and hot-desking area has added a new social dynamic to the office community here. It provides our members with a space for the exchange of ideas and to meet and network, which is so important to developing companies.

Most visitors are struck immediately by the uniqueness and playfulness of the space and the contrast between Dogpatch Labs and a traditional working environment. The concept of co-working is novel to Ireland and some visitors can take a while to get used to it. However, most acclimatise after a few visits, myself included, to the point where it's hard to imagine working in another environment.

57

Ekimetrics

Paris, France

Ekimetrics, an innovative marketing and data consultancy firm, was created in 2006. Their office was completed in 2014 and is located in a nineteenth-century building on the Champs-Élysées.

Design: Vincent & Gloria Architectes
Photography: Arnaud Schelstraete

The building is a nineteenth-century *classé* palace with golden mouldings and frescoed ceilings. The concept was to play with these constraints and break the codes of standardised office spaces by creating places that reflect the innovative team spirit.

The scale of the office spaces is large, with 1,000 square metres and five-metre-high ceilings. It gave us the opportunity to create sub-spaces in raw wood. The choice of raw material is deliberate to create contrast and also to respect budget constraints. The chance to design the identity of the office, from architecture to furniture, is a unique opportunity to create the right culture.

What we love about our new offices is the way the wooden structures create a strong identity in contrast to the heritage of the building, conveying our culture and our way of not taking things too seriously. We also love the way common spaces create natural links within the team: the architecture is not just for projecting a good image, it is part of our way of living and working.

Clients are surprised and amazed by our offices. They see how dynamic and innovative we are and they feel they are in a truly creative environment. They feel part of a special culture and history and they often ask to organise workshops and meetings here.

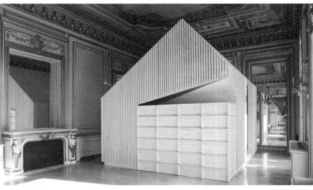
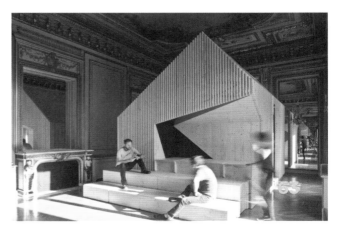

Filter017

Taichung, Taiwan

Since 2004, Filter017 has worked on a wide variety of projects, including graphic design, packaging, photography, installation art, clothing, accessories, toys, skateboards and even locomotive modification.

Design: Filter017
Photography: Highlite Images

We decided to apply an industrial-style decorating theme, using a cement floor with cement walls and exposed iron pipes with a special design. We tried to use the iron and cement elements to reconcile cold-tone elements such as the wood, white wall and blackboard.

We love our vintage toy collections and interesting books, and the stress-relieving green plants, which make us feel well. Because the brand has been in operation for many years, we still have our favourite items from each period and place those pieces in our workplace to show the unique working atmosphere. We also have two cats, a favourite among colleagues.

The whole workplace really shows our brand's individuality. In this cold space you feel warm and cosy, because of the colourful and vintage elements.

FIVE AM

Kortrijk, Belgium

FIVE AM is a design studio specialising in creating concepts ranging from interiors and temporary installations to product design. Their main workspace is located in the centre of Kortrijk and this renovated caravan is used as a mobile office.

Design: FIVE AM
Photography: STØR

As a design office, we had been thinking about a mobile space for a long time, so we bought an old caravan. But then we didn't have the time to design it, so it stayed in my backyard for two years.

#dojowheels is a mobile training facility, or dojo, as a working tool, which is a perfect reflection of our vision. It can easily change its setup to offer the user the most practical surroundings. The flat surface acts as a bed, a couch and a table, with storage available underneath.

We especially like the functional and flexible wall. Every time we meet in #dojowheels we can change its function. Sometimes we use it as a canvas for a big floor plan; sometimes we use it as a storage wall for pens and paper – the wall adapts according to our needs at that moment.

Fold7

London, England

Fold7 is a creative advertising agency that was founded in 1995 by Simon Packer and Ryan Newey. Their abstract 650-square-metre offices were designed by fellow Londoners Paul Crofts Studio, and the project was completed in 2015.

Design: Paul Crofts Studio
Photography: Hufton + Crow

The Fold7 office concept was a melding of several themes. We wanted to create 'classy with a twist': a welcoming feeling, the sort you'd find at a boutique hotel, blended with a sense of playfulness and fun to create a 'rug pull' on what you first feel. We're in the imagination game, after all.

There are various great features and details scattered through the building. I especially like the details, language and phrases scattered around the corners, under chairs, on ceilings, in surprising places. My single favourite part of the building is actually the overall effect. For a creative agency there has to be a connected way of working and an environment which contributes to creative thinking. Moving around the office, sitting in different spaces and getting different outlooks gets the brain working differently.

Oh, and the hidden door in the bookshelf, very James Bond. Everybody wants one of those, don't they?

73

74

All visitors are met with the large message 'WELCOME TO THE FOLD' featured behind reception. It's more than a few token words, it's a genuine open hand reaching for a warm greeting.

Future Deluxe

London, England

Future Deluxe is an experimental creative studio driven by research, technology and the pursuit of new aesthetics and techniques. Their studio is located in London.

Design: 44th Hill
Photography: 44th Hill

Our work in the studio is very digital and technology-based, so, to mix it up, the warmth of reclaimed wood and hundreds of festoon light bulbs felt like a very good mix.

I have so many favourite things about the workplace! I love the meeting room and the reclaimed sliding industrial doors, as well as the handmade table made from coloured reclaimed wood. And let's not forget our very own Mary! 'Electric Holyland' is a commissioned piece from Brighton-based neon and light artist Andy Doig.

The studio is a great talking point for clients and visitors – although many initially think we must be some religious design cult, due to the crucifix and statue.

BORN IN BRIGHTON
MADE IN LONDON

The studio is a great talking point for clients and visitors – although many initially think we must be some religious design cult, due to the crucifix and statue.

Ganna Studio

Taipei, Taiwan

Built in 2013, Ganna Studio is not merely a workplace but also a cosy home for two designers. In this 53-square-metre house in central Taipei, the designers have implemented a traffic line to divide living and working spaces.

Design: Ganna Design
Photography: MWphotonic

The design concept was to create a home and workplace together. In crowded Taipei, we need to make the best use of every corner of the house. We need to work and live here, therefore the design started with the traffic line – we try to prevent people in the house from being bothered by each other. Five revolving panels were adapted as a partition between the dining and working area, helping people work independently. When the panels are open, sunlight can be let into the inner house.

We like the living room the most, as it can be used as a showroom when we have clients or visitors in the house. The wall in the living room can also reflect the beautiful red door in daytime, and present the shadow projected by the chandelier. The living room is not only a place for us to relax, but also a stage for the light and the shadow.

We always dreamt of having a place where we could work and live, so we took all the details into consideration while designing our studio. In a word, Ganna Studio is small but perfectly formed.

Ghostly Ferns

New York, USA

Ghostly Ferns is a family of freelance creatives located in the Gowanus neighborhood of Brooklyn. Their workplace is in the attic of a townhouse which houses three additional storeys of other freelancers.

Design: Homepolish
Photography: Claire Esparros

We call our attic the Haunted Attic of Ghostly Ferns because it's surely haunted by all of the plants we've killed during our time here. We wanted the design of our space to be light and airy, with mostly black, white, wood, marble and tons of plants. Our work is very clean, yet personable, and we really wanted our space to reflect that.

The best part about our workplace is the people. Sure, our attic is small, but we wouldn't have it any other way. The five Ghostly Ferns are all best friends and we have the best time being packed tightly in our tiny attic. We laugh until we cry daily and take loads of long lunches together.

Clients are always dumbfounded as to how we work together successfully in such a small space. When they find out just how well we get along, they're even more surprised. It's often hard for people to fathom a healthy working relationship in such a small space, but we love it this way. Clients are also usually impressed by our poop emoji pillow on our sofa, which we've appropriately named 'the poop sofa'.

Homepolish

New York, USA

Homepolish is a tailored interior design service set up in 2002 by Will Nathan and Noa Santos that aims to deliver stylish and affordable design services to all clients. Its office is located in New York City, and the interior is made up of partitioned spaces that were created without using a single wall.

Design: Noa Santos & Shelly Lynch-Sparks
Photography: Claire Esparros

We designed the space around mobility. We wanted to create small spaces where teams could break out into groups and conceptualise or brainstorm together – both comfortable and functional. We kept the style and aesthetic clean and modern to reflect the brand.

Our favourite thing about our workplace is our living plant wall and the greenhouses we converted to conference rooms. Clients and visitors love the space. The first comment we usually get is related to the lighting and how grand the space feels.

"HELL, THERE ARE NO RULES HERE - WE'RE TRYING TO ACCOMPLISH SOMETHING."

-EDISON

How do you approach designing offices for creative clients?
We start with the brand and design to bring it to life by giving the space personality that reflects functionality and form.

Be the
Solution

Dream
Smart

Keep
it Fun

89

Hvass&Hannibal

Copenhagen, Denmark

Nan Na Hvass and Sofie Hannibal, graphic
designers and illustrators, set up their studio in
2006, and have been in Frederiksberg since April
2013. The space is 140 square metres divided into
five rooms and a kitchen.

Design: Hvass&Hannibal

Photography: Chiara Dal Maso/Hvass&Hannibal

The concept was that it should be like a second
home, with all the books and trinkets (like two plastic
volcanoes) that we're not allowed by our husbands to
have at home. We wanted it to be a working studio, with
our stuff on the walls and with room for our posters,
leftover material from projects, fabric, wood pieces,
cardboard tubes and all our books. We rarely use any of
it, but it's nice that it's there.

Our favourite thing is the built-in loft bed/
bookcase! The ceiling is four metres high, so it seemed
like a good idea to build a floor-to-ceiling bookshelf with
a loft bed in the middle where you can take a nap if work
gets too overwhelming. We talked and dreamed about
this for years, but it wasn't until we found this office
space that it was actually possible to build it. It was
envisioned by us and built by Bo Benzon and his team.

Visitors say they want to move in! Or stay and
drink tea at least. They think it's a very creative, personal
and cosy environment. Our new studio mate Daniel
Frost says it's pretty much perfect and we think so too.

INC Architecture & Design

New York, USA

Incorporated is an open source, multidisciplinary
architecture and design studio, with experience in
a wide range of project types, that specialises in the
integration of the design disciplines. The studio has
been located in Lower Manhattan for two years.

Design: INC Architecture & Design
Photography: David Heald

Our home is our castle. INC's new studio is a portrait of
our aspirations and our culture. The goal was to create an
environment that embodies the values of our company.
Comfortable, casual, solid and refined were to be its
hallmarks. The space was stripped back to its essential
architectural shell of unfinished brick, simple concrete
and raw plaster. The maple floors were stripped, painted,
buffed and bleached to bring out their natural and
honest beauty. Our space is filled with collected bespoke
materials, objects and details inspired by our projects,
our wanderings and our passions.

Music is a big part of our day. We find that it cuts
tension, provides an acoustical buffer in the open studio
context and generally lubricates the day. Everyone
controls the playlist. Sometimes there are playlist wars,
but generally there is a collective consensus that the
mornings are mellow, the middle of the day is a little
more upbeat, and in the later evening, when the day's
meetings are over, the volume goes up.

We are on a high floor and are lucky enough to
be surrounded by lower buildings. Some days, when
the sun is at just the right angle, you feel like you are at
30,000 feet.

Ippolito Fleitz Group

Stuttgart, Germany

Ippolito Fleitz Group is a multidisciplinary design studio founded by Peter Ippolito and Gunter Fleitz in 2002. Their 480-square-metre office in Stuttgart was designed by the company and completed in 2008.

Design: Ippolito Fleitz Group
Photography: Zooey Braun

Our studio is situated in a former factory for control technology in the west of Stuttgart. The five-storey Gründerzeit building was originally constructed at the turn of the last century to house an industrial laundry. Largely reconstructed after the war due to heavy bombing damage, the first floor of the building retains something of its original character as a production facility. The four-metre-high ceiling is supported by cast-iron pillars, a feature rarely found in Stuttgart, giving the space a nostalgic feel. With a floor area of almost 500 square metres, the studio provides the necessary space for free, creative thinking.

The nucleus of our office is the studio. Here, people from different design disciplines work on projects in concert. The open-plan interior was specifically selected to encourage cross-pollination and creative intercourse, fostering an interdisciplinary design process.

Reflecting the studio's conceptualisation as 'identity architects', our premises were designed as a quasi-signature trademark for clients and studio staff alike.

Jelly Button & Hamutzim

Tel Aviv, Israel

JellyButton, a mobile games company founded in 2011, and Hamutzim, a digital design studio founded in 2005, share an eclectic 700-square-metre workspace in Tel Aviv. Designed by Roy David Studio, it was completed in 2015 and occupies an industrial loft-style building in the south of the city.

Design: Roy David Studio
Photography: Yoav Gurin

The overall concept draws its inspiration from the surroundings of the building, which is located in an area of south Tel Aviv that is well known for its 'low-fi' industrial urban style. The main design idea was to create a three-segment plan of public, semi-public and private areas. It resembles the ripple effect, with the public space standing in the core, serving as a knowledge-sharing centre, inspiring interaction between the office's various professionals. The minimal industrial and eclectic design reflects the office's culture, which aspires to perfection, creativity and joyfulness.

Jen Clark Design

Melbourne, Australia

Jen Clark Design is a branding, graphic and web design studio based in Collingwood, Melbourne.

Design: Jen Clark Design
Photography: Brent Lukey

We wanted a space that would welcome and inspire us on a daily basis, as well as tangibly demonstrate our design ethos to clients, guests and passers-by. Our colourful, engaging workspace uses a variety of sustainable materials sourced by local suppliers, and is inspired by industrial and Scandinavian design principles.

We love that our studio was completely designed by us, for us. It's spacious and light-filled and suits our needs perfectly. Being surrounded by the work of local designers, artists and talented tradespeople provides us with daily inspiration. We believe the best advertisement for a design firm is their own office and we're pretty proud of ours.

Visitors to our studio regularly comment on its design. They particularly love the charcoal walls and the bold contrast these create with our extensive library of reference books, long white desktops on trestle legs, vibrant artwork and custom-made bar that doubles as a room divider.

Jennet Liaw

Portland, USA

Jennet Liaw is a full-time designer and freelancer, who spends her days at the Nike World HQ and works from home at night on freelance design projects.

Design: Jennet Liaw
Photography: Jennet Liaw

Taking photos, editing and designing are constant activities here, so it was a priority to design a space that inspires productivity, yet also allows for repose. I chose a layout that has a tiny cell of a bedroom, tucked away behind a sliding door. I keep this purely private space void of electronics and other potentially stressful elements. The rest of the floor plan is minimal, focused on the functionality of the various surfaces for designing, crafting and brainstorming.

Aesthetically, the entire unit is definitely a continuation of my personal taste in graphic design as well as fashion – I love to push monochrome using natural textures and shapes. I first fell in love with the space itself for its concrete walls and high ceilings; however, it was innately quite dark and serious, so I paired the existing industrial feel with light, organic elements and clean lines.

We're located in the Pearl district of Portland, which is a budding hotspot of urban renewal, so the uniqueness of the surrounding reclaimed warehouses and railroad yards truly sets the scene for creativity.

Lehrer Architects

Los Angeles, USA

Michael B. Lehrer founded Lehrer Architects in his native district of Los Feliz as a sole proprietorship in 1985. Twenty-six years later, the business, now a California corporation, is still thriving in the award-winning office space at 2140 Hyperion Avenue.

Design: Lehrer Architects
Photography: Benny Chan Fotoworks & Lehrer Architects

Our studio was created on a shoestring budget with succinct architectural interventions – it fosters fluid movement between colleagues, our work stations, our model-building and our creation of art. We use our R&D Room for making objects that feed back into the inspiration of the office, because we believe making is a primal pleasure. We also host life drawing for the community once a month, among other events, such as weddings, fundraising galas, book readings, film screenings and concerts.

The openness of our studio design allows mentors and protégés to communicate freely. The red stripe on our inexpensive, epoxy floor heightens awareness of space and the unusual shape of our warehouse. Luckily, the library and service space are sunlit all day long, honouring their critical nature to our work. The patio extends our indoor/outdoor sightlines through a light-dappled bamboo garden that we use on a daily basis.

The quality of light that streams through the ample skylights reminds us how privileged we are to make beauty. We rarely use artificial light, and are blessed with a climate that ushers in a breeze through our open garage doors to compliment the generous sunlight.

Louise Fili

New York, USA

Founded in 1989, Louise Fili Ltd is a graphic design studio located in Manhattan specialising in brand development for food packaging and restaurants.

Design: Louise Fili
Photography: Louise Fili

My graphic design studio has been located in a repurposed apartment near Gramercy Park in Manhattan for close to eight years. For the over twenty-five years that I have had my own business, I've always kept my office in the neighbourhood so that I can walk to work. I prefer to work with smaller businesses, run by owners whom I genuinely like and whose products I respect – and consume! There is always excellent wine, gelato, jams, crackers, biscotti, chocolate and coffee on hand.

My studio is a walk-in archive of all the restaurant menus, business cards, matchbooks and specialty food packages I have designed, as well as the many posters and flea-market finds I have gathered from years of travelling in Italy and France. Surrounded by objects that I treasure, I always feel at home.

We have a wonderful kitchen. I feel just as comfortable cooking lunch for staff or clients as I do designing. We have two gelato clients, so the freezer is always well-stocked. I make a point of scheduling meetings for the afternoon, and serve gelato first. It's hard not to love that.

121

Lundgren+Linqvist

Gothenburg, Sweden

Founded in 2007, Lundgren+Lindqvist is a design and development studio based in Gothenburg. The current studio, which has been the company's home for the last three years, is located on the top floor of Sockerbruket, an old sugar factory situated on the harbour front of the city.

Design: Lundgren+Lindqvist
Photography: Hannes Ahremark

We have striven to combine the feeling of a creative workshop and a more home-like environment. In short, a place where you will gladly spend a few extra hours after work, if not working on a client project then perhaps to experiment on a self-initiated project, to read a book or to play a game of table tennis.

Our studio is located on the top floor of an old, brick-clad sugar factory, which today houses a myriad of creative businesses, artists and photographers. Looking out through our windows, we overlook Gothenburg's harbour front, with its industrial landscape and giant cargo ships docking to unload their containers.

As our studio is centrally located, yet not in the absolute heart of the city, many of our clients prefer having meetings here, as opposed to their own offices. Seeing that we also have a great collection of paper samples and reference objects, not to mention delicious coffee, it makes discussing design projects easier.

We overlook Gothenburg's harbour front, with its industrial landscape and giant cargo ships docking to unload their containers.

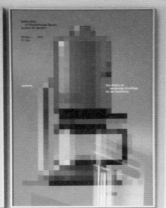

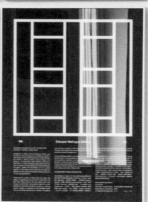

Fumer nuit
gravement à **votre**
santé et à celle
de **votre** ent**ourage**

...t was set in FS Emeric ExtraLight by Extra Light
...esigner, Anna Iversén, who is 14 years old and
...w days with Lundgren+Lindqvist during a field trip
...rite colour is green.

127

Mamiya Shinichi Design Studio

Nagoya, Japan

Mamiya Shinichi Design Studio is an architectural firm that was established in 2006. Their suburban Nagoya office occupies 250 square metres across numerous different levels, and was built in 2013.

Design: Mamiya Shinichi Design Studio
Photography: Toshiyuki Yano

Our work is designing architecture and real estate. Every day, we have meetings with clients and conferences at the office in the morning.

We got the idea from the safari park. There are no fences in the safari park. We considered that if we could work in a free atmosphere, we would be able to develop our personalities and it would be better for creating good ideas.

It is quite useful for having events like symposiums here. It is easy to make a platform and audience seats because the space can hold lots of people and there are different floor levels.

Our clients seem to be quite surprised when they come to our workspace. And then they praise us: 'This workspace makes you create many great ideas!' Furthermore, they tell us the different ceiling heights and floor levels have the charm of variety, and they enjoy walking around the office.

Mattson Creative

California, USA

Mattson Creative is an award-winning graphic design studio that creates visual language for vibrant brands. SND CYN Studios is located in a former factory in Southern California.

Design: SND CYN Studios
Photography: Rod Foster, Josh Elliott, Lauren Hillary

Mattson Creative is a small design firm, by design. The only downside of running a boutique studio is that you really don't need that much space to do it. I've always wanted to work in a big, ultra-creative office – an inspiring environment, teeming with interesting people, doing inspiring work. But I've never wanted to manage the number of employees that would necessitate a studio of that size. My passion is design, not management. I wanted the energy, community and culture of a large creative agency … I just didn't want the agency.

So I set out to create the type of office that I wanted to work in, and I invited my friends and colleagues to join me. It turns out that they were looking for the same thing I was: a unique environment and a creative community. I decided to expand our existing space in Old Town Irvine into a collaborative workspace for creative professionals. We filled it quickly and now the space is home to artists, designers, photographers, producers and developers. And I get to go to work every day with my friends. We call it SND CYN Studios – which is derived from our address on Sand Canyon Avenue.

MER

Stockholm, Sweden

MER is a leading architecture and consultancy firm located in Stockholm that specialises in offices for Swedish and international companies.

Design: MER
Photography: Mårten Ryner

Our office is a creative workshop and the concept is built around 'exhibition'. Our office design showcases, illustrates and supports our workdays. We have used a lot of different materials, colours and methods, both to inspire us as architects and to have a showroom for clients. Our office is our laboratory and is under constant reconstruction. We've also worked a lot with the layout and located the fundamental office features in different parts of the space to encourage activity, flexibility and inspiration. From a design perspective, the most eye-catching thing is either the polished steel room-dividing wall or the paper cube.

Visitors tend to be surprised by how an office layout can be used as a strategic tool from a business perspective. They also love the idea of not having your own desk, that you choose where you want to work depending on today's task or mood of the day. Today, our office is one of our best marketing tools.

Mono

Minneapolis, USA

Mono is an advertising and branding agency located in the Uptown neighbourhood of Minneapolis. The eleven-year-old agency moved into the current workspace in 2012.

Design: Charlie Lazor & Alex Haecker
Photography: Mono

We view our workspace as a tool, carefully designed to facilitate how we work and how we create. The most distinctive feature in our space is a massive wall that is literally the heart of the agency. We have no offices or private workspaces. We all simply work collaboratively and openly at the wall. There, people from different disciplines come together to provide unique perspectives that allow us to develop innovative creative ideas to solve our clients' business challenges.

In our kitchen we have a massive wooden table, affectionately nicknamed Woody, which serves as a warm, welcoming gathering space for us all. The forty-foot table is constructed from a single tree, creating a continuous, natural surface.

When people come to our space for the first time, they look as if they have just emerged from a dark and dreary tunnel and are now flooded with openness and light. The space radiates optimism, collaboration and creativity, and people's reaction to it is visceral. Our clients often choose to travel to our office for meetings, as well as attempt to replicate elements of our workspace within their own existing offices.

142

competitive

QSR behaviors

Naja Tolsing

Copenhagen, Denmark

Naja Tolsing is a Danish collage artist, graphic designer and architect with a personal workplace established in 2010 in the centre of Copenhagen.

Design: Naja Tolsing
Photography: Naja Tolsing

The whole idea of having a home office is to work but not think of it as work! As a designer I'm always searching for solutions or systems, but as a collage artist there is no defined finish line and all decisions are based on emotions. My home is the perfect setting for this very personal process.

I think that the collage art suits my home and that a visit to my home office gives people more perspective on me and the world of my collages. Most people like the atmosphere here, and the people who are less interested in the story behind the artwork tend to shop online instead.

What do you love about your workplace? Everything! The evening light. The fact that I only need a couple of magazines, a scalpel, some glue and some nice paper. And of course music and coffee...

149

Nicholas Tye Architects

Bedfordshire, England

Nicolas Tye Architects has been trading for over twelve years and focuses on residential and commercial high-end architecture and design, driven by its founding architect Nicolas Tye.

Design: Nicholas Tye Architects
Photography: Philip Bier

The concept behind the studio is deeply embedded in creating a building that sits well within the context of its surroundings and is an inspiration to its users and visitors alike. The context of the building is that it sits adjacent to some historical barn/farm structures which are made from timber and rusty metal details. It also sits adjacent to trees and woodland. The solution is a simple twenty-first-century interpretation of the 'barn' in a modernist timber-clad and metal-edged detail solution which responds to its adjacent buildings and natural surroundings.

The calm open-plan spaces, luscious light and vast swathes of glazing mean that the outside of the room is an is an ever-changing seasonal feast for the eyes. All of this leads to a high-end commercial solution that provides the optimum inspiration to its employees and visitors.

Nova Iskra

Belgrade, Serbia

Design incubator Nova Iskra is a co-working space for design professionals and a meeting point for creative professionals and companies who would like to advance their business by using creative potential.

Design: Milica Maksimović & Aleksa Bijelović
Photography: Relja Ivanic

We are an open co-working space with a focus on the fields of design and creative industries. The idea is to provide a professional and fully functional workspace for emerging creative professionals from Serbia and the Balkans, but also to host contemporary nomads who are visiting Belgrade and are on the lookout for a temporary workspace.

Our favourite thing about our workplace is the wide mix of people and disciplines that are present in the space, as we are not a typical IT start-up co-working space, as well as the magnificent interior designed by our friends and members from Studio Petokraka.

The reactions are extremely positive, especially from the people who are using the space daily. They enjoy the calm and focused atmosphere, the mellow music and the social aspect of working here. From the very start, the intention was that the space should reflect the ideas and mission behind Nova Iskra, and we believe that this is very much the case with everyone who visits us for the first time. That is also why many of our members manage to develop their business or careers from here, and why Nova Iskra as an organisation manages to grow and expand its circle of partners, clients and collaborators.

155

The idea is to provide a professional and fully functional workspace for emerging creative professionals ... but also to host contemporary nomads.

Ogilvy & Mather

Tokyo, Japan

Ogilvy & Mather is one of the largest marketing
communications companies in the world and
Ogilvy & Mather Japan was established in 1995.
The company is comprised of industry-leading
units in the following disciplines: advertising;
public relations; branding and identity; shopper
and retail marketing; direct, digital, promotion and
relationship marketing; consulting and analytics;
branded content; and specialist communications.

Design: Ogilvy & Mather
Photography: Ogilvy & Mather

We renovated our office in 2014. Prior to our renovation,
our company was divided into six departments, each
with its own entrance and thick walls that separated
them. Within each department we had built cubicles that
were around five feet tall, which added an additional silo
and prevented staff from seeing each other and having
natural conversations. This inhibited idea-sharing, casual
discussions and collaboration across disciplines. We
addressed these issues by knocking down the walls and
scrapping the cubicles, and built an entirely open-plan
space which encourages collaborations.

We wanted to inspire and stimulate our staff so
we commissioned some local Japanese artists and
photographers to produce unique art that brings to life
some of Ogilvy's values, such as courage, persistence
and playfulness. So there is now beautiful art all around
the office that inspires the staff and our visitors. Funky
art, interesting furniture, cool breakout spaces – these
small touches go a long way toward changing the
mindset of the staff.

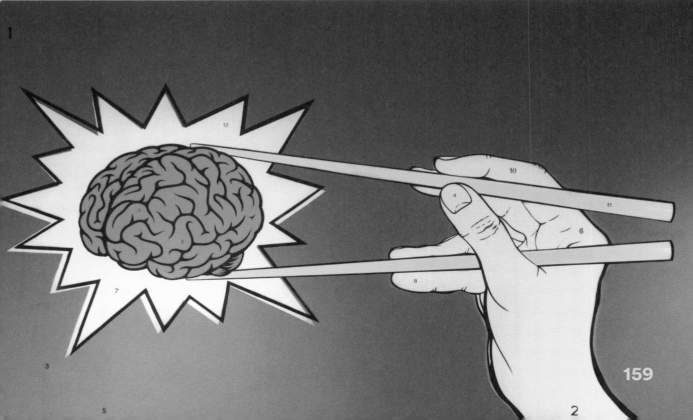

159

Oktavilla

Stockholm, Sweden

Oktavilla is a team of strategists, designers
and developers working in mostly long-term
relationships with clients. Their office is housed in
an old textile manufacturing hall on Södermalm,
and in 2009 Elding Oscarson was contracted to
redesign the space.

Design: Elding Oscarson

Photography: Åke E:son Lindman

We loved the naked, lofty and bright spaces here and
wanted to keep the beautiful industrial atmosphere,
but needed to alter it drastically to make it operable
for our business.

Dividing the space with a wall gives a very bright
and large meeting room, as well as a clean rectangular
room for the rest of the program. This large space is
softly divided with a box containing service functions
and a kitchen. By compressing the contents of the
box and positioning it very carefully, the scheme
effortlessly falls into place without breaking the
impression of a single large room. The magnetic
cladding of galvanised steel picks up the colours of the
surroundings in a hazy reflection and further defines
the box as an inserted element.

Besides having a literal relevance to where we
are coming from (we used to design magazines), the
wall made of stacked bundles of magazines is not only
a natural conversation piece in its mere irrationality,
but also works as an acoustical absorbent.

Largely, the raw, untreated space was kept
untouched after demolition to keep the beauty of an
industrial atmosphere. By adding only two clearly
defined architectural elements the space is reinforced.
The lighting solution and interior design also aim at
highlighting the nakedness of the space.

Park + Associates

The Herencia, Singapore

Having moved out of a typical office building, Park + Associates were searching for a new space that would not just accommodate their expansion but also reflect the philosophy of their creative pursuits. The architects' office today occupies the mezzanine level of an old school building in Singapore's River Valley enclave.

Design: Park + Associates
Photography: Edward Hendricks

This site is a former school compound which was built in the 1960s. The school was vacated in 2001 and the building was subsequently converted into a commercial development in 2013. Our workspace is located where the old library hall used to be. Situated at the highest part of the building, it contains an expanse of column-free space crowned by a series of barrel vaults.

Seeking to celebrate and activate the intrinsic qualities of the existing space, the scheme is conceived as an orchestration of varied and contextually sensitive spatial experiences instead of the function-centric approach typical of office design. It dovetails with the design direction, which rejects the rigidity of the typical bureau in favour of a creative environment that challenges conventions and celebrates informal spaces – an Anti-Office.

This approach creates seamless informal spaces where functional boundaries become ambiguous. The employees feel more liberated in their creative work as a result of the casual and relaxed office environment.

Random Studio

Amsterdam, The Netherlands

Random Studio's office is situated on the Westzaanstraat in Amsterdam. It has been around for more than ten years and has evolved from a production studio into an interactive design studio working with an international team for international progressives.

Design: X+L Architects
Photography: Kasia Gatkowska

The concept for the design was to create an open space but at the same time allow for a visual division so there is some sort of privacy, allowing people to work in project teams. Furthermore, we like the light and obviously the plants do too. The plants allow for nature to be present – it feels somehow right and less like work this way. The indoor garden, the mirror monolith and the bags filled with plants hanging from the ceiling give the space an edge. I like that. It's not just a garden. It's a bit unusual, and because the plants grow the place constantly changes. That's what we want with our work as well. Constant change.

The studio *is* constantly changing: we are changing project teams, we have different freelancers coming in, we are building different things in the studio itself and are changing the decoration. So the whole studio feels alive, always changing…

Because the plants grow, the place constantly changes. That's what we want with our work as well. Constant change.

Red Paper Heart

New York, USA

Red Paper Heart is an art studio composed of designers and coders who work together to combine interactivity and animation. They have been based in their current space in Brooklyn for a little over two years.

Design: Tina Apostolou, Homepolish
Photography: Christina Shields

At Red Paper Heart our work is focused on blending the digital with the physical and so our space needed to represent that as well. The office is split between desks and computers, a prototype area and areas where we can sit and collaborate. Our favourite thing about the office is the prototype area – it's amazing to be able to get up from your screen and create something physical, as well as come into the office in the morning and see what someone built the night before. It's a place of constant creation and inspiration.

When we chose this space we knew that while it wasn't huge, it was raw enough for us to grow and test. Our typical day starts with us all huddled around the espresso machine and from there we are spread out between working on prototypes, coding and designing.

178

reMIX Studio

Beijing, China

reMIX Studio is a young office based in
Beijing, born from the experience that
the three founding partners – Chen Chen,
Federico Ruberto and Nicola Saladino – have
developed during years of academic research
and collaborations with various international
firms, working on multiple design scales.

Design: Chen Chen, Federico Ruberto & Nicola Saladino
Photography: reMIX Studio

The space is an internal, unexpected 'foreign body'
that integrates and absorbs all the irregularities of
pre-existing structures and materials. It is arranged
as a series of screens; planes of different opacities
that render each point of view a unique sequence of
successive spatial differences.

The subtle changes of colour and constantly
varying shadows are one of its most peculiar, and
hence one of our favourite, features. Another of our
favourite aspects is how the space manages to reach
scalar alternation and variation thorough the interplay
of material transparencies.

Visitors usually comment on the way cold and
newly inserted materials are coupled with pre-existing
ones – how the contrast between the roughness of
the brick walls and the slick irregularities of the steel
surfaces nicely echo each other.

Ricardo Bofill Taller de Arquitectura

Barcelona, Spain

More than fifty years after its foundation, Ricardo Bofill Taller de Arquitectura remains at the forefront of the urban design and architectural professions. The third-generation family business is located in a former cement factory on the outskirts of Barcelona.

Design: Ricardo Bofill
Photography: Lluis Carbonell

Seduced by the contradictions and the ambiguity of the place, I decided to retain the factory and, modifying its original brutality, sculpt it like a work of art. It is for me the only place where I can concentrate, associate ideas in the most abstract manner, and finally create projects, images and new spaces, and constitute a specific vocabulary for our architecture.

Visitors are amazed by the grandeur of the spaces and the mixture of old and new. They feel transported to an unfamiliar environment. I have the impression of living in a closed universe which shields me from the outside and everyday life. The Cement Factory is a place of work *par excellence*. Life goes on here with very little difference between work and leisure.

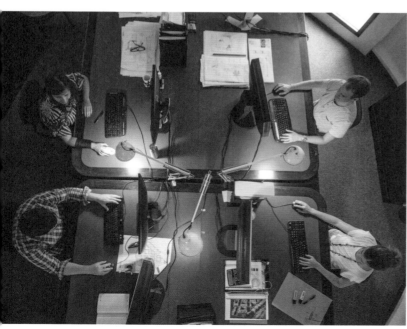

selgascano

Madrid, Spain

selgascano is an architectural partnership between José Selgas and Lucía Cano. Their subterranean offices are situated amongst downtown Madrid's trees.

Design: selgascano
Photography: Iwan Baan

What we sought to do with this studio was quite simple: to work under the trees. To do so, we needed a roof that was as transparent as possible. Also, we needed to isolate the desk zone from direct sunlight. Hence the transparent northern part, the part that is covered with a bent sheet of 20mm colourless Plexiglas. The south side, where the desks are, had to be closed in much more, but not completely, so there is a double sheet of fibreglass and polyester in its natural colour on the south side, with translucent insulation in the middle. All three form a 110mm-thick sandwich.

Everything placed below ground level is in concrete with wood formwork; wooden planks are also used for paving, firmly bolted and painted in two colours with two-component paint with an epoxy base.

And to finish off, we have given it a wet touch, with the sound of the raindrops hitting the plastic on rainy days.

Schneid

Lübeck, Germany

Schneid is a design studio focused on formal purity, functionality and a minimalist approach, and their workplace is in the historic city of Lübeck. In 2014, they restored an old metal industry training workshop to create their 400-square-metre studio.

Design: Schneid
Photography: Noel Richter

Our intention was to combine this old, industrial interior with our own contemporary designs. When we rummaged through the left-behinds of the former training workshop, we discovered great furniture that we could easily restore by giving it a fresh lick of paint. But we also felt that it was important to keep the original spirit of this space, so we renovated all of the beautiful old windows and didn't simply replace them with new ones. It was our aim to have a big, open and bright room, where we would be able to work and spend our free time.

We have everything together in one building. We have our workshop next to our kitchen. When we go upstairs we can relax on our roof terrace. This way, our workspace serves not only as our office, but also as our workshop, photo studio, showroom and warehouse.

Our workspace is located outside the city centre, so we don't have any passing customers. People come specifically to see this old building and how we use it – sometimes from totally different backgrounds: some are design lovers or clients, but there are also former trainees that were taught in the workshop. It's interesting to hear their stories about the place: it reminds us of its history.

Spaces Architects

New Delhi, India

Kapil Aggarwal graduated from MIT, Manipal, in 1996 and worked for three years with reputed architectural firms before setting up his own practice. Spaces is based in New Delhi and is laid out over 150 square metres.

Design: Kapil Aggarwal
Photography: Bharat Aggarwal

The whole thought process of designing this studio was based on three major criteria.

The first was personal. When I say personal, the process of creating the office space was influenced by my journey through different experiences and practices over the years. The second was intended for the people who visit the office without any predefined notion, to feel the space and to experience the firm's ideology. The third and the most important factor was the people working in the space. A lot of emphasis was placed upon what they require – a place where they can feel good and that is comfortable to work in.

The most interesting part was an experiment in designing the main cabin outer partition in a fluid form with veneer cladding which continues to the conference room ceiling. The partition is inclined on both the planes and takes an interesting form. The conference room and cabin have a glass sliding and folding partition which when pulled creates an individual space.

The office design was conceived to be a place where being at leisure is also conducive to a creative environment: a workplace to enjoy.

Studio Boot

Den Bosch, The Netherlands

Studio Boot is a graphic design studio that was founded in 1991 in 's-Hertogenbosch by Edwin Vollebergh and Petra Janssen. The studio has been based in its current premises for two years.

Design: Piet Hein Eek, Hilberink Bosch Architecten
Photography: Jean-Marc Wullschleger

We live and work in the same building, a former car repair shop in the centre of an old town. It is one of the few industrial buildings left. The design studio is situated at the front of the building – the plan is very similar to the original plan of the garage as it may have been. It's big, open and bright – a great place to work and live. We like to live in our working space and work in our living space – we like our work!

You can never have enough space: it's a luxury. And we have a big kitchen area, big enough for groups, and a big garden. The backyard of the building looks like a farm, a farm situated in the heart of town.

Everybody loves it; people are surprised when they enter, overwhelmed by the light and space. It's great to work here!

Studio Output

London, England

Studio Output is a branding, design and digital agency. All aspects of strategy are covered here and they have been in this area of East London for several years.

Design: Jackdaw Studio
Photography: Studio Output

A typical day in Output towers sees us start early with a giant pot of tea, plan the day in lively group meetings and then spend the day creating everything from visual identities and marketing campaigns through to digital products and brand strategies.

We took a purple and orange 1990s partitioned horror show of an office and ripped everything out. We then brought back elements of the building's character (we're in an old piano factory) like the old steel lift doors and brickwork, and bought a more organic feel to it with oak flooring and wooden wall panels (which are recycled Victorian floorboards). We then dressed it with examples of our work, prints from artists we collaborate with and the odd splash of bright colour – which is something you see in all our work.

You get some great sunrises here in the morning and if you stick your head out the window you can see St Paul's, if you're lucky.

You get some great sunrises here in the morning and if you stick your head out the window you can see St Paul's, if you're lucky

213

Superheroes

Amsterdam, The Netherlands

Superheroes is a digitally born and raised international creative agency based in Amsterdam with services that span the globe.

Design: Simon Bush-King Architecture & Urbanism
Photography: Alan Jensen

Our main aim was to get maximum impact in a space where we only had a three-year lease. We looked for a careful balance of pragmatic needs for a functioning agency while projecting a strong character. The studio is constructed with high-tech means but low-cost and tactile materials with OSB, grey felt, glass and lots of plants used throughout.

Our superhero llama is by far the most famous fixture of our space but everyone who works here has a different thing they love about the hideout. The swing is very dear to us, but it continues to be a polarising feature. Lauded by some as a great place for phone calls, it inspires maternal feelings of concern in others.

First-time visitors to our office have an immediate and instant reaction when walking into the space. Jealousy. There's always a moment of mock-outrage as they reflect on their own boring, llama-less office. After this, they just want to explore the space. The open floor plan, hanging plants and natural light give a sort of playground-for-adults feel, and visitors instantly act the part.

TOS Estudio

Madrid, Spain

TOS is a creative studio established in 2013 in the dynamic neighbourhood of Lavapiés. It is a studio-workshop focused on exploring new concepts and techniques across multiple disciplines.

Design: TOS Estudio
Photography: TOS Estudio

We were looking for a space that would allow us to meet our handcraft expectations, and fortunately we found it. TOS is a two-level space with a basement that holds a screenprint workshop and a photography studio. Here, we can create our very own limited print productions, carve some wood or run a staged photoshoot.

TOS is situated in a cosy street at the heart of the artistic hub in Madrid. We are at street level, which allows us not only to be more in touch with the street and people around us, but also to be part of the commercial vibe of the area, next to art galleries, bars and neighbourhood associations. In addition, the studio is surrounded by four big windows to exhibit our designs, a privileged space to have real contact between our work and the people outside.

Visitors always love the studio; it's packed with art, emotions and a clear organic interior design. Handmade furniture and screenprints decorate the different spaces, together with the original inner walls from the nineteenth century. TOS is situated right next to the Reina Sofia Modern Art Museum, an area packed with history and creativity with a tremendous artistic atmosphere, which immerses our visitors in the contemporary trends the area has to offer.

What is the concept behind your workplace's design? To get our hands dirty again.

Wieden+Kennedy

New York, USA

Wieden+Kennedy is an independent, integrated, full-service agency with strategy, creative, interactive, media planning and buying capabilities and services. W+K was founded in Portland, Oregon, in 1982 and the New York office opened in 1995.

Design: WORKac
Photography: Tony McAteer

We all agreed we didn't want anything that felt gimmicky. It's one of the things that happens at a lot of agencies. It's easy to fall into the 'we're-so-fun' trap. For us, the people that work here will be the ones to bring that personality; it didn't need to be the concern of the architecture. We wanted to create something timeless.

The Coin Stair, the main staircase that connects the sixth and seventh floors, is really the focal point of the agency. It doubles as a mini auditorium where we hold our all agency meetings. The bar at the top of the staircase is a close second though.

It's always humbling when visitors come into our space. It's easy to take it for granted when you're here every day, but when a client or a group of students, for example, comes in to see the space for the first time, you feel their sense of inspiration instantly. It's always a welcome refresher.